LOOKING AT LITERATURE

MY FIRST LOOK AT FOLKTALES

BY ROSIE BANKS

Please visit our website, www.garethstevens.com. For a free color catalog of all our high-quality books, call toll free 1-800-542-2595 or fax 1-877-542-2596.

Library of Congress Cataloging-in-Publication Data

Names: Banks, Rosie, 1978- author.
Title: My first look at folktales / Rosie Banks.
Description: New York : Gareth Stevens Publishing, 2022. | Series: Looking at literature | Includes index and webology. | Audience: Grades 2-3
Identifiers: LCCN 2020028210 (print) | LCCN 2020028211 (ebook) | ISBN 9781538263990 (library binding) | ISBN 9781538263976 (paperback) | ISBN 9781538263983 (set) | ISBN 9781538264003 (ebook)
Subjects: LCSH: Tales–History and criticism–Juvenile literature.
Classification: LCC GR74 .B36 2022 (print) | LCC GR74 (ebook) | DDC 398.2–dc23
LC record available at https://lccn.loc.gov/2020028210
LC ebook record available at https://lccn.loc.gov/2020028211

Published in 2022 by
Gareth Stevens Publishing
111 East 14th Street, Suite 349
New York, NY 10003

Designer: Rachel Rising
Editor: Kate Mikoley

Photo credits: Cover, p.1 Larissa Kulik/Shutterstock.com; pp. 3, 4, 6, 8, 10, 12, 14, 16, 18, 20, 21, 22, 23, 24 (background) carduus/DigitalVision Vectors/Getty Images; p. 5 Image Source/Getty Images; p. 7 Universal History Archive/Universal Images Group/Getty Images; p. 9 Culture Club/Hulton Archive/Getty Images; p. 11 Slava Gerj/Shutterstock.com; p. 13 Floridapfe from S.Korea Kim in cherl/Moment/Getty Images; p. 15 GraphicaArtis/Archive Photos/Getty Images; p. 17 API/Gamma-Rapho/Getty Images; p. 19 CSA-Printstock/DigitalVision Vectors/Getty Images; p. 20 Bloomberg/Getty Images; p. 21 Mohd Safwan Abd Rahman/EyeEm/Getty Images.

Printed in the United States of America

CPSIA compliance information: Batch #CSGS22: For further information contact Gareth Stevens, New York, New York at 1-800-542-2595.

CONTENTS

Boldface words appear in the glossary.

Telling Tales

Stories are an important part of every **culture**. Long ago, people didn't read and write. They told their stories aloud. Others remembered them and told them too. These stories were passed down over many, many years. Some are called folktales.

Cloudy
Windy
Days of the Week
Sunday Sun.

Folktale Features

Folktales are fictional. That means they aren't true. They may even have magic or talking animals in them. Fairy tales and **fables** are kinds of folktales. No one knows who made up most folktales because they're so old.

"The Three Little Men in the Wood"

There are often many **versions** of a folktale because so many people have told them. Every storyteller tells a story differently. Many folktales have a moral, or lesson. Others try to explain something. Some are just a fun story!

"Goldilocks and the Three Bears"

Tricksters

Native American cultures passed down many folktales. A lot of these tales feature tricksters. Tricksters are characters that play tricks on others. Sometimes they're animals. The **raven** is a trickster in folktales from native peoples of the Pacific Northwest.

A South African Tale

Some folktales explain something. The Zulu people of South Africa told a tale explaining why cheetahs have black face markings. The tale said that a mean and lazy hunter stole a mother cheetah's cubs. She cried so much that all cheetahs now have tear marks.

The *Arabian Nights*

The *Arabian Nights* folktales come from the **Middle East**. They're more than 1,000 years old. Aladdin, Ali Baba, and Sinbad the Sailor are *Arabian Nights* heroes. They weren't rich or powerful, but they did amazing things. Folktales are often about regular people.

"Ali Baba and the Forty Thieves"

A Russian Folktale

Folktales were used to teach sometimes. Baba Yaga is a magical woman in Russian folktales. She helps people who are **humble** and smart. She **punishes** those who aren't. Baba Yaga stories taught Russian children how they should act.

Baba Yaga

An American Folktale

Some folktales are set in a certain area. Paul Bunyan folktales take place in the United States. Bunyan's size and strength were **exaggerated**. He was said to have made hills, lakes, rivers, and other natural features! Exaggerated folktales are also called tall tales.

Paul Bunyan

Favorite Folktales

Your favorite stories may come from folktales. Perhaps they began as a folktale and became a movie, like *Aladdin*. Even if you think you know a folktale, reading another version can be fun. Imagine all the storytellers who have told it over the years!

Your Turn!

Write a short folktale about someone who finds a **treasure**. Tell it to a friend. Ask your friend to tell it to someone else. You're passing on a folktale!

GLOSSARY

culture: the beliefs and ways of life of a group of people

exaggerated: larger or greater than real life

fable: a short story often about animals that teaches a lesson

humble: not believing you are better than other people

Middle East: the area where southwestern Asia meets northeastern Africa

punish: to make someone suffer for wrongdoing

raven: a black bird that is larger than a crow

treasure: something of great value that is often hidden

version: a form of something that is different from others

FOR MORE INFORMATION

BOOKS

Baker, Tom. *50 Famous Fables and Folk Tales: Collected from Around the World*. Atglen, PA: Schiffer Publishing, 2016.

Palmer, Kate Salley. *The Lady of Cofitachequi: A South Carolina Native American Folktale*. Columbia, SC: University of South Carolina Press, 2019.

WEBSITES

African Folktales
anikefoundation.org/african-folktales
Check out more African folktales here.

Children's Literature
georgiasouthern.libguides.com/c.php?g=838319&p=5987833
Find valuable definitions here.

Native American Indian Legends and Folklore
www.native-languages.org/legends.htm
Read this large collection of folktales.

Publisher's note to educators and parents: Our editors have carefully reviewed these websites to ensure that they are suitable for students. Many websites change frequently, however, and we cannot guarantee that a site's future contents will continue to meet our high standards of quality and educational value. Be advised that students should be closely supervised whenever they access the internet.

INDEX